Meet the Hawaiian Menehunes

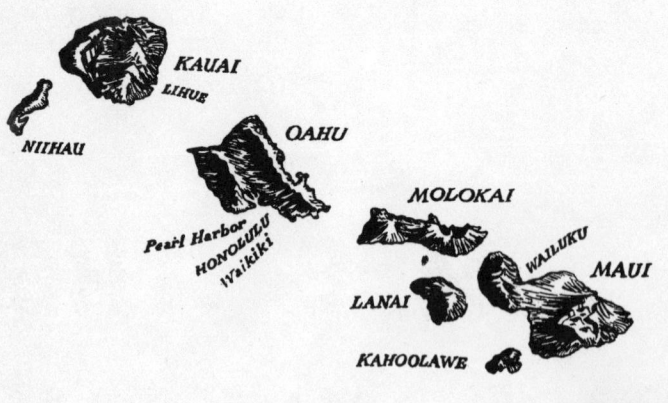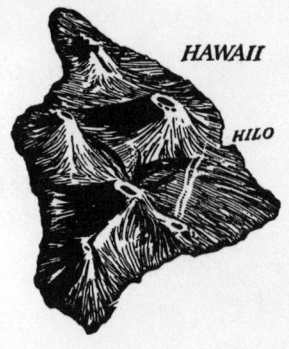

Vivian Laubach Thompson

MEET THE HAWAIIAN MENEHUNES

THE PETROGLYPH PRESS
HILO STREET 96720
201 KINOOLE HAWAII

ALL RIGHTS RESERVED

COPYRIGHT © 1952, 1967 BY

VIVIAN LAUBACH THOMPSON

PUBLISHED BY THE PETROGLYPH PRESS

4th Printing

ISBN 0-912180-08-0

ART CONSULTANT, CHRISTINA LOTHIAN

MANUFACTURED IN THE UNITED STATES OF AMERICA

DEDICATION

*To the two people
who made this book possible:
Odessa Davenport . . . and Dan . . .*

Acknowledgement

I should like to take this opportunity to say *mahalo a nui loa* to Ezer K. Mathews for his generous *kokua* in compiling the glossary of Hawaiian words.

My thanks also to Donald F. Duncan, Inc., for permission to use their registered trademark Yo Yo in the story of "The Menehune's Yo Yo."

Foreword

To Children Everywhere,

If you visit, or read about, Hawaii, you will soon hear of menehunes, the little folk of the Islands. Stories about them have been handed down from the days of Old Hawaii.

They were strong little men and hard workers, building great stone walls in a single night. They were good at sports: diving, swimming, running. They were fond of games: top spinning, tumbling, tug-of-war. And how they liked to eat! Their favorite foods were shrimp, small fish called silver-sides, and pudding made of taro and coconut.

Menehunes were seldom seen by daylight. They did their work at night, and any job that could not be finished before dawn was left unfinished. They could be kind and helpful, or mischievous **and full of tricks.** They could bring good weather if given a small gift, or send fog and rain if laughed at.

Wonderful tales are told about menehunes of other days. What of menehunes today? Many people who have lived in Hawaii for years will tell you they have never seen one. Why? That's simple. Menehunes are invisible unless you believe in them. But children can see them! Here are some stories of children who did see menehunes. Won't you come and meet them, too?

Vivian L. Thompson

CONTENTS

Foreword

THE NIGHT OF THE SEVEN SPLASHES 1
a story of how the Hawaiian Islands might have been built by the menehunes: Eka, Peka, Luka, Oka, Kele, Moke, and Wene.

CHOCOLATE PUDDING FOR THE MENEHUNES . . 10
in which Kikokiko, Eleele, and Melemele discover that they like chocolate pudding even better than Kulolo.

THE MENEHUNE'S YO YO 21
Palani learns some top tricks from a menehune and teaches him how to use a Yo Yo.

MENEHUNE MIKO 30
a menehune helps Miko make friends in the new school where he is the smallest boy in second grade.

THE DAM THAT DISAPPEARED 36
Teo, a timid young camper, finds courage to speak out to a menehune chief.

Glossary 43

The Night of the Seven Splashes

Once upon a time, in old Hawaii, on the island of Kauai, there lived seven menehunes. Not only seven, of course. Kauai was the home of the menehunes so the island was crowded with them. Among them were seven special menehunes. Their names were Eka, Peka, Luka, Oka, Kele, Moke and Wene.

Eka was energetic, a good rider and very fond of horses and cattle.

Peka was a quiet, studious fellow, very fond of books.

Luka was a careless fellow who always looked as though he needed a bath.

Oka was a hungry fellow ... always eating pineapple.

Kele was a lazy fellow. He liked to sit and doze by the side of a stream with a bamboo fishing pole in his hand. If he caught a fish, that was fine. If he didn't, that was even better—for then there was nothing to disturb his nap.

Moke was a friendly fellow. He liked noise and crowds and meeting new people.

Wene was just the opposite. He *disliked* noise and crowds and meeting people. All he wanted was to be left alone.

Now, the menehunes were very busy people. They built fishponds and strong sea walls. They worked always at night and no matter how great the task, it was finished in one night or not at all.

One day, the King of the menehunes sent word that a new wall was to be built and all the menehunes would be needed.

"Auwe!" said Eka. "I planned to round up my cattle!"

"Auwe!" said Peka. "I planned to finish the book I am reading!"

"Auwe!" said Luka. "I planned to do nothing at all. If I work on the sea wall, I'll get dirty and have to take a bath. You know how I hate water!"

Oka tried to say "Auwe!", but his mouth was full of pineapple. When he finished it, he said, "I planned to work in my pineapple field!"

"Auwe!" cried Kele. "I planned to go fishing!"

"Auwe!" cried Moke. "I planned to meet some people!"

"Bah!" snorted Wene. "There will be crowds of people there tonight! I hate crowds!"

The seven menehunes were silent for a moment. Then Eka spoke. "It seems to me the time has come for us to move. Kauai is getting too crowded. We all have special things to do and there is never enough time to do them."

"That's right," said Peka. "Why don't we speak to the King about it tonight?"

"That's a fine idea!" said Luka. "You're the best speaker, Peka. You tell him."

"Very well," Peka agreed.

That night, when the seven menehunes reported to the King for work, Peka told the King how they felt. The King listened soberly until Peka had finished, then he studied the faces of the seven.

"I have known you for a long time," he said, "and I am sure you are not suggesting this just to get out of work. Kauai *is* getting crowded. This may well be the time to spread out and you may be the very ones to start. Help us finish this sea wall tonight. Tomorrow night we shall help you find new places to live."

The following night, when the menehunes were gathered together, the King made his announcement. "For many years, the island of Kauai has been growing more and more crowded. Seven menehunes have asked permission to find new places to live. Our task tonight will be to help them build new islands."

A gasp went up from the menehunes. New islands! They had undertaken many difficult tasks but none as difficult as this! The King waited for the crowd to quiet down.

"Until tonight," he continued, "there has been but one island—the island of Kauai. After tonight there will be eight islands making up Hawaii. Each of our seven friends will have his own island. On it he may live alone or invite others to join him."

"But how can we build new islands?" one of the menehunes asked. "We can never carry enough stones in one night to build seven islands!"

The King smiled. "There will be no need to carry stones," he said. "You are forgetting our strongest helpers, the Volcano and the Sea. For many years they worked together to build the island of Kauai. Since then they have built up many new layers of lava. Now it is just beneath the surface of the water. All we need to do tonight is to pull it up! Bring our strongest ropes! The most skillful divers gather over here! The best swimmers over there! To work, everyone!"

Never was there such a busy night in the history of Kauai! The divers tied ropes about their waists and dove into the blue waters of the Pacific. They tied the ropes to jutting pieces of lava beneath the water. Swimmers carried the ends of the ropes to menehunes on shore. Here they were fastened to one huge rope. The King gave the signal. "Huki!" he shouted. "Huki!"

Along the shore, hundreds of menehunes lined up in a great tug of war. At first, nothing happened. The strong menehunes continued to pull until suddenly, with a huge splash, a mass of lava came to the surface. They continued pulling until an island larger than Kauai appeared.

"Fine!" said the King. "Now, which of you seven would like this island for your home?"

"If my friends do not object," said Moke, "I would. Here I could invite many people to join me. We could build a bustling city that people would come from far away to visit."

"Is that agreeable to the others?" asked the King.

"Ae," the six agreed.

"Then cast loose the ropes," the King ordered.

The divers dove beneath the water to loosen the ropes. But some of the menehunes, impatient to get on with the night's work, tugged too soon. With a deafening crack, a piece of the new island flew into the air and landed with a splash a short distance offshore.

The King looked very stern and was about to scold the impatient menehunes but Wene spoke up.

"If you please," he said, "that small piece would just suit me. No one else would care to live there so I could live alone, as I prefer."

"Very well," said the King. "That makes our work simpler. We have only five more islands to finish now. Come, everybody! On to the new island! We shall continue our work from there!"

With a lusty shout, the menehunes dove into the water and swam to the new island. The King and his attendants followed in his outrigger canoe.

From the new island the process was repeated. At the signal "Huki!" the menehunes pulled and tugged with all their might. With a splash, a narrow strip of lava broke the surface.

"Who would like to make his home on this island?" the King asked.

"I would like it," replied Kele. "It has many fine spots along its shores that could be made into fishponds."

So it was decided that this should be Kele's home. Once again the menehunes dove into the water and swam to the new island. As soon as the King's outrigger arrived, the work began again.

The pulling seemed much harder this time. Eka, Peka, Luka and Oka began to think the menehunes would grow weary before enough islands were found for them all. They knew if the job was not finished that night, the menehunes would not return to it.

At a splash, they discovered what had made the work so hard. The island that appeared was larger than Moke's island . . . so large that no one could see the opposite end of it.

"Four of you left," said the King. "Who wants this island?"

"I would like it," said Peka. "It has much fine coral. From it I could build a school and teach others to love books as I do."

"Very well," said the King. "Let's get on with the job."

The menehunes churned the water into froth as they dove once more and swam to Peka's island and began work again.

This time, though the menehunes pulled and tugged

with all their might, they could not bring the newest island to the surface.

"We must try harder," urged the King. "I promised these men new homes tonight and already the sky is growing light. Once more now, everybody!"

With many grunts and groans, the menehunes tugged until a tip of lava appeared at last. It rose higher and higher until the newest island towered above the others. With an enormous splash, the biggest, highest island any of the menehunes had ever seen came to the surface.

"Well done!" said the King. "No wonder you had a hard time pulling this one up! Those peaks rising in the center are Mauna Kea and Mauna Loa—two volcanos! Choose quickly now. We have two more islands to go."

"This would be a fine place to raise horses and cattle," said Eka. "May I have it?"

"Yes," said the King. "Now, let us hurry to provide Luka and Oka with homes."

But before the menehunes could set out again, they heard with dismay the sound of a cock crowing far back on Kauai.

"There will not be time to fish two more islands from the sea before daybreak," said the King sorrowfully. "Luka and Oka, what do you wish us to do?"

"I should be happy with just a small piece chipped off Eka's island," said Luka. "All I want is a place where I can be as dirty as I please with no one to tell me to take a bath!"

"Very well," said the King. "On to the Big Island! Bring the hammers!"

Again the water boiled with menehunes swimming

for the Big Island. As the outrigger touched the shore, some jumped out carrying hammers and picks. They began pounding at the rocky floor of the Big Island.

The sky grew lighter and lighter and the menehunes worked faster and faster. Suddenly there was a loud crack and a chunk broke away from the shore and flew into the air. It traveled with such force that it burst in two in mid-air. When the two huge splashes had calmed down, there in the Pacific lay two new small islands.

"That solves our problem!" Oka shouted joyfully. "I shall take the second piece. All I want is a small place to raise pineapple."

"Splendid!" said the King. "You have all done a fine night's work, men, and have finished not a bit too soon. Now, let us be off to our homes before the sun finds us here."

With a happy shout, the menehunes plunged into the water for the last time that night and swam furiously for Kauai. Eka, Peka, Luka, Oka, Kele, Moke and Wene went to their new islands.

As the sun peeped over the horizon, it shone down on a chain of eight islands where there had been but one the day before.

Is this story true? Who can say? But this, I do know. There are eight islands making up Hawaii today and they seem to have turned out much as the menehunes planned them long, long ago.

Oahu, the island Moke chose, contains the bustling city of Honolulu and hundreds of people come every year by boat and plane to visit.

Niihau, the island on which Wene chose to live alone, remains that kind of island to this day. It is the only island in the Hawaiian chain which no one may visit without an invitation.

Kele's island, now called Molokai, is a friendly, sleepy little island with many fine fishponds.

The island Peka chose is known as Maui. Anyone can tell you the first school west of the Rockies was built on that island.

Eka's island, Hawaii, even today is called the Big Island. It contains one of the largest cattle ranches in the world.

And the two pieces chipped from the Big Island? Oka's island, called Lanai, leads today in the raising of pineapple. Luka's island, Kahoolawe, is deserted. Not even Luka lives there! But perhaps he got his wish, and never had to take another bath. You see, the reason no one lives there is because there is no water on that island!

Chocolate Pudding for the Menehunes

The sun dropped lower in the sky as Pilipo climbed higher and higher up the woody mountain trail. The sack slung over his shoulder was nearly full of long green strands of the fragrant maile vine. As soon as he filled it, he would start home to strip the vines and twist them into long, sweet-smelling leis . . . one for his mother, one for his grandmother, Tutuma, and one for jolly Mrs. Poepoe who lived next door.

Soon the light in the woods grew dim. Pilipo could hunt no longer. He hung the last strand of maile around his neck and started back along the trail. It was hard to see in the dim light. Somewhere he took the wrong turn. Suddenly, Pilipo realized he was lost.

"Auwe!" he exclaimed. "A fine thing! I was born at the foot of this mountain trail. Yet here I am lost like a small keiki without his mother! Now if there were a menehune around to show me the way...."

"Just a minute...." called a small voice. The leaves at the side of the trail rustled. In the dim light Pilipo saw a little man wearing a brown polka-dotted malo. About his neck hung a lei of orange hibiscus and he had tucked one hibiscus blossom behind his ear.

"Well, who are you?" asked Pilipo.

"I'm Kikokiko. You called for a menehune, didn't you?" asked the little man.

"Yes, I did, but I really didn't expect to find one," said Pilipo.

"Well, do you need one or not?" asked the little man, a trifle crossly. "Menehunes are busy people. We haven't time to waste."

"I do need help," Pilipo admitted. "I've been gathering maile and I've lost my way. Could you help me find the trail down the mountain?"

"Ae," said Kikokiko. "Wait, I'll call my brothers. Eleele!"

"Ele-ele," Pilipo repeated softly. "That means black. That's a strange name...."

Out from the leaves beside the trail came another little man. He looked like the first menehune but his malo was black. He wore a lei of red hibiscus and one red blossom tucked behind his ear. He turned and called over his shoulder, "Melemele!"

"Mele-mele . . . yellow," Pilipo thought. He watched eagerly to see if the next little menehune would be wearing yellow.

He was! His malo, his hibiscus lei and the blossom tucked behind his ear were all yellow.

"This is Pilipo," Kikokiko explained. "He has lost his way. We must help him find the trail down the mountain."

"We'll need torches," said Eleele.

"We'll get them," said Melemele.

Both menehunes disappeared into the woods again. Soon they were back carrying three flaming torches. Eleele, Melemele and Kikokiko each took a torch. The little procession started down the mountainside with Pilipo. With the torchlight to guide him, Pilipo was soon back on familiar ground.

"I can find my way from here," he said. "Mahalo a nui loa. Is there anything I can do to repay you?"

"No, I don't think so," said Kikokiko, smiling.

"There is too! There is too!" shouted Eleele, jumping up and down.

"The Kulolo! Ask him about the pudding!" squealed Melemele, clapping his hands.

"Pudding? What about pudding?" Pilipo asked.

"We are very fond of Kulolo," Kikokiko explained. "As you know, it is a pudding made from taro and coconut. But up here, we cannot raise taro or coconut so we have no way to make Kulolo. We do miss it."

"Could you get us some taro?" shouted Eleele, jumping up and down.

"Could you make us some Kulolo?" squealed Melemele, clapping his hands.

"I don't know," said Pilipo, "but I'll certainly try."

"That's very kind of you," said Kikokiko.

"I'll come tomorrow and let you know," Pilipo promised. "Where can I find you?"

"Take this," said Kikokiko. He handed Pilipo a small koa whistle. "It's a menehune whistle," he said. "Just blow it whenever you want us. We can hear it no matter how far away we are."

"Mahalo," said Pilipo. "I'll take very good care of it. Aloha. I'll see you tomorrow."

It was late when Pilipo got home. There was no time to talk about his strange adventure. Next morning at breakfast, he said, "Mother, why don't we ever have Kulolo? You used to make it."

"When we lived out in the country, we had our own taro patch," said his mother. "Now we live in the city. One cannot grow taro in a flower pot."

"No, that is true," Pilipo agreed.

After breakfast, Pilipo wandered next door. Mrs. Poepoe, their plump, jolly neighbor was working in her garden.

"Your husband has a taro patch, hasn't he?" Pilipo asked.

"Ae. He does," Mrs. Poepoe answered. "That is where he is now. Early this morning he drove out to the valley to work in his taro patch."

"Will he be back tomorrow?" Pilipo asked eagerly.

"Tomorrow? No," said Mrs. Poepoe. "He is staying all week end there."

"Oh," said Pilipo, disappointed. He wandered back to his house. On the front lanai sat his grandmother, stringing a lei of plumeria blossoms.

"Tutuma," said Pilipo, "where can I get some Kulolo?"

"I don't know," said Tutuma slowly. "Not many people in the city make it. Why do you ask?"

"I want it for some friends of mine," said Pilipo. "They helped me find my way home last night when I lost the mountain trail. They are very fond of Kulolo."

"Would your friends happen to be menehunes?" asked Tutuma, her eyes twinkling.

Pilipo looked startled. "How did you know?" he gasped.

Tutuma smiled. "Don't forget, I was born on the island of Kauai, the first home of the menehunes. I know how much they like Kulolo."

"What shall I do?" Pilipo asked. "I don't want to disappoint them."

"If I were a boy about your age and with the name of Pilipo, this is what I would do," said Tutuma. She whispered in Pilipo's ear and the two disappeared into the kitchen.

Soon after lunch, Pilipo started out for the mountains. In his arms he carried a big covered calabash. In his pocket he carried a box. When he reached the foot of the trail, he set this bowl down carefully on a flat rock. Taking the small koa whistle from his pocket, he blew a tiny, shrill blast.

Soon, the leaves beside the trail rustled and out

popped Kikokiko. Behind him came Eleele followed by Melemele.

"It is good to see you again," said Kikokiko smiling.

"Did you find some taro?" shouted Eleele, jumping up and down.

"Did you make some Kulolo?" squealed Melemele, clapping his hands.

"No," said Pilipo. "I couldn't find either one. I've brought you something else instead."

"What is it?" asked Kikokiko.

"It's chocolate pudding," said Pilipo. "Let's sit down and try it." He reached into his pocket and took out the box. From the box he took four paper dishes and four red plastic spoons.

"You pass these please, Kikokiko, while I serve the pudding," said Pilipo.

Eleele and Melemele sat down cross-legged and Kikokiko handed them their dishes and spoons. Pilipo came around with the bowl and spooned chocolate pudding into each dish. When Kikokiko had his dish, Pilipo served himself.

"Taste it," said Pilipo. "See if you like it."

Three spoons dipped into the pudding.

"It's . . . very dark," said Eleele, cautiously.

"It's . . . very sweet," said Melemele, doubtfully.

"It's very good!" said Kikokiko enthusiastically. "I like it very much!" He dipped his spoon again.

Eleele dipped his spoon and took another taste. "It's not *much* darker than Kulolo," he said slowly.

Melemele dipped his spoon and took another taste. "It's not *much* sweeter than Kulolo," he said quickly.

Eleele's spoon dipped faster and faster until his dish was empty. Melemele's spoon dipped faster and faster until *his* dish was empty. When Kikokiko and Pilipo had finished their pudding also, Pilipo stood up.

"It was very kind of you to bring us the chocolate pudding," said Kikokiko.

"Come and see us again," shouted Eleele, jumping up and down.

"If you have any left-over chocolate pudding, we'll help you finish it," squealed Melemele, clapping his hands.

Back home the days passed and Pilipo had almost forgotten about the menehunes until strange things began happening.

"Auwe!" cried his mother one evening. "I made chocolate pudding for dessert tonight. Now the pudding is gone and in its place is a basket of shrimp!"

"Are they fine shrimp . . . plump and fresh?" Pilipo asked.

"Ae. They are," his mother agreed. "But who ever heard of eating plump, fresh shrimp for dessert?"

The next morning, Mrs. Poepoe came running to Pilipo's house.

"Auwe!" she cried. "I made some chocolate pudding as filling for a birthday cake. Now the pudding is gone and in its place is a basket of shrimp!"

"Are they fine shrimp . . . plump and fresh?" Pilipo asked.

"Ae. They are," Mrs. Poepoe agreed. "But who ever

heard of a birthday cake with plump, fresh shrimp for filling?"

That afternoon, the ladies of Tutuma's sewing circle came to work on their Hawaiian quilt. When it was time to serve refreshments, Tutuma came running out to the lanai.

"Auwe!" she cried. "I made some chocolate pudding for sauce for our ice cream. Now the pudding is gone and in its place is this basket of shrimp!"

"They are very fine shrimp . . . plump and fresh!" said one of the ladies.

"Ae. They are," Tutuma agreed. "But who ever heard of ice cream with plump, fresh shrimp sauce?"

When the ladies of the sewing circle had gone, Tutuma called Pilipo. "This is the third time chocolate pudding has disappeared, Pilipo," she said. "I think you'd better go see your menehune friends again."

"But what can I tell them?" Pilipo asked. "They meant no harm."

"Perhaps if you show them how to make their own pudding, they will stop taking it from others," said Tutuma. "There are six boxes of chocolate pudding mix on my pantry shelf. You may take those to the menehunes. That should last them for quite some time. Perhaps you can think of something for them to do when those are gone."

"Mahalo, Tutuma," said Pilipo.

As Pilipo started out the door with the six boxes under his arm, Tutuma called to him.

"Better take them this old cooking pot," she said. "I know how careless men are about cooking!"

When Pilipo reached the foot of the mountain trail, he set the six boxes on the flat stone with the cooking pot beside them. He took the little koa whistle from his pocket and blew a tiny shrill blast.

Soon the leaves beside the trail rustled and out popped Kikokiko. Behind him came Eleele followed by Melemele.

"My friends," said Pilipo, "strange things have been happening in my neighborhood. My mother makes chocolate pudding for dessert. It disappears and a basket of shrimp is left in its place. Mrs. Poepoe makes chocolate pudding for a birthday cake. It disappears and a basket of shrimp is left in its place. Tutuma makes chocolate pudding as ice cream sauce . . . and what happens?"

"It disappears and a basket of shrimp is left in its place!" said Eleele and Melemele in chorus.

"Then you do know about it!" said Pilipo.

"Yes," Kikokiko admitted. "They took the pudding. It smelled so good they just couldn't resist. They thought the folks might not mind if they left the shrimp in exchange."

"They were very fine shrimp! The ladies liked them very much, but it wasn't what they had in mind for dessert!" Pilipo said, laughing. "I've brought you some packages of chocolate pudding mix so you can make your own."

"Hurray!" shouted Eleele, jumping up and down.

"Yippee!" squealed Melemele, clapping his hands.

"You will need a fire," said Pilipo.

"Ahi . . . fire. We can make that," said Kikokiko.

"A cooking pot . . . " Philipo continued. "Tutuma sent one for you . . . two cups of milk. . . ."

"Waiu . . . milk?" Kikokiko repeated doubtfully. "We are too high in the mountains to raise cows. Where can we get milk?"

The three menehunes looked very sad.

"Niu!" shouted Eleele, jumping up and down.

"That's right! Coconut milk!" squealed Melemele, clapping his hands.

"But coconut palms do not grow this high either," said Kikokiko.

"Along the beach!" shouted Eleele.

"Where we go for shrimp!" squealed Melemele.

"Fine!" said Pilipo. "Then you will be all set. When you are ready, open one package. Pour the powder into the pot. Add two cups of milk. Stir and cook over the fire until it thickens. That's all there is to it. These six packages should last you for quite a while. When they are gone, I have another idea."

"What is it?" Kikokiko asked eagerly.

"The shrimp you catch are very fine," said Pilipo. "Plumper and fresher than ours. When you need more chocolate pudding, take a basket of fresh shrimp down to Mr. Kalepa, the storekeeper in the village. I have spoken to him about it."

"Yippee!" squealed Eleele, so excited that *he* clapped *his* hands!

"Hurray!" shouted Melemele, so excited that *he* jumped up and down!

"Mahalo a nui loa," said Kikokiko. "You are our good aikane, Pilipo. We shall meet again."

One evening several weeks later, Pilipo, his mother and Tutuma were sitting on the front lanai. Mrs. Poepoe came over to join them.

"Those were very fine shrimp we had for supper," said Tutuma. "Where did you get them?"

"From Mr. Kalepa," said Pilipo's mother. "I asked him where he got such plump, fresh shrimp and he made a little joke. He said the menehunes brought them!"

"That is funny," said Mrs. Poepoe. "I went into Mr. Kalepa's store today for chocolate pudding. He had none. I asked him what happened to all the chocolate pudding he had on his shelf yesterday. He said the menehunes took it!"

"I think Mr. Kalepa likes to tease," said Pilipo's mother.

"Don't forget," said Tutuma, "Mr. Kalepa comes from the island of Kauai. Maybe he *believes* in menehunes!"

Tutuma looked at Pilipo. Pilipo looked at Tutuma. They grinned.

The Menehune's Yo Yo

Palani wandered through the woods, frowning. As he walked he spun his red Yo Yo. He did the Breakaway, the Pin Wheel and Hop the Fence but his mind was not on the tricks.

Palani was thinking about the playground contest. He wanted to enter the top-spinning competition. The trouble was that he knew very little about top spinning. His specialty was Yo Yo tricks and there was no Yo Yo competition in the contest.

Bending down, he made the Yo Yo do The Creeper, watching it idly as it crawled the length of the string along the leafy trail. As he jerked it back, the string caught in an overhanging twig and the Yo Yo rolled off into the weeds. He stooped to pick it up and was surprised to find the string had tangled with another string. He tugged and his eyes popped open as he felt a tug on the other end. He backed up, pulling steadily. Slowly the string came toward him. The leaves beside the trail began to rustle and a tiny voice squealed, "Let go! Let go! It's not yours!"

Palani gave a last tug and there, at the other end of the string, stood a tiny little man dressed in a green malo. He looked very indignant indeed.

"Let go!" he cried again. "It's my top string, not yours!"

Palani dropped the string in surprise. "Why, you're a menehune!" he exclaimed.

"Of course I'm a menehune," said the little man, "and this is a menehune top. It wouldn't do *you* a bit of good. You couldn't make it work unless I showed you how."

Palani looked at the top in the little man's hand. It was very unusual. It was made from a kukui nut, smoothed and polished until it shone like black glass.

"That's a beauty!" said Palani. In his excitement he dropped his Yo Yo.

The menehune glanced at the Yo Yo on the ground. "What kind of a top is this?" he asked. "It has no point. How can you make it spin?"

"This is a Filipino top called a Yo Yo. It doesn't need a point. It spins on the string. I'll show you." Rewinding the string, Palani swung his arm at his side and did a Three Leaf Clover.

The menehune's eyes followed the little wooden toy as it made three graceful loops.

"That's very good!" he said.

"Now you show me a trick with your top." Palani suggested.

"Very well," said the menehune. He wound his top carefully. With a quick twist of his wrist he sent it spinning into the air then caught it on his open palm. It spun there steadily. "Huli!" he called and flipped his hand over. The top continued spinning on the back of his hand. "Hele mai," called the menehune softly. The little top began spinning slowly up the back of his hand, across his wrist and up his arm. As it neared his elbow the menehune gave another command. "Hoihope!" Obediently the top backed up, traveled down his arm, across his wrist and on to the back of his hand again. "Huli!" the menehune repeated and flipped his hand over. The top finished its spin on his palm.

"Well, that's the best top spinning I've ever seen!" Palani declared.

"It should be," said the menehune. "Menehunes are the best top spinners and I'm the champion menehune spinner. That's how I got my name."

"What is your name? Mine is Palani."

"My name is Niniu Nui. It means Great Top Spinner. I'm called Niniu for short."

"Niniu, I wish I could do that trick! I could certainly win a prize in the playground contest if you taught me!"

"We'll make a bargain," said Niniu. "I will teach

you some menehune top tricks if you will teach me some Yo Yo tricks."

"Fine!" said Palani. "Will you show me how to make a kukui nut top like yours, too?"

"Ae. Go find some kukui nuts and bring back a file and some fine sandpaper," said Niniu. "Can you bring a Yo Yo for me, too?"

"Of course," said Palani. "I'll be back right after lunch."

Soon after lunch, Palani was back with a blue Yo Yo for Niniu, six kukui nuts, a file and sandpaper. When he reached the spot where he had met the menehune that morning, he called, "Alo—ha, Nini—u!"

"Alo—ha, Pala—ni!" came an answering call in the distance.

Soon the leaves beside the trail rustled and out popped Niniu.

"Did you bring my Yo Yo?" he asked eagerly.

"I certainly did," said Palani, "a blue one."

"Show me how to start!" cried Niniu, delightedly. "I can practice while you are filing your kukui."

"All right," said Palani, taking the Yo Yos from his pocket. "First you must learn to wind it correctly. It does not wind like a top. Hold it in your left hand and spin it up the string a little way. Then when you move your right hand up and down, it will bring the Yo Yo up to your hand. When you have learned how to wind it, I will show you how to throw a Spinner."

"Let me try!" said Niniu. He looped the string over his middle finger and holding the Yo Yo in his left hand, tried to spin it up the string as Palani had directed. The Yo Yo jumped out of his fingers and dropped to the ground . . . klunk!

"Auwe!" said Niniu. "Not so good!"

"It takes time," said Palani. "Just keep at it. But first, show me how to start on my kukui nut. Then you can practice while I am working."

Niniu looked over the six kukui nuts carefully and chose the one that balanced best on his palm. "Take your file," he said, "and smooth down all the bumps and ridges. How soon is the contest?"

"Next Saturday," said Palani. "A week from today."

"We shall have to work every day at this," said Niniu, "to finish it in time to learn some tricks."

An hour passed while Palani filed away and Niniu practiced spinning. The kukui began to lose its bumps. It began to take on a rounded shape.

"I'll work on this some more at home," said Palani. "What do I do next?"

"You sand it, going always in one direction," said Niniu. "Tomorrow you must bring ulu blossoms."

" Ulu blossoms!" Palani repeated. "What for? I'm making a top, not a lei!"

"I know that!" said Niniu, laughing. "The flower petals will smooth out the scratches."

"I never knew that!" said Palani. "Now let me help you do a Spinner before I go."

Sunday morning, Palani was back with his kukui nut and the ulu blossoms. "How is your spinning coming?" he asked.

"Maikai!" said **Niniu eagerly**. "**Last** night I got four out of five spins!"

"Good work!" said Palani. "You can learn the Breakaway today."

The morning hurried by while Niniu practiced his new trick and Palani smoothed out scratches with the ulu blossoms. "What do I do next?" Palani asked, when it was time to leave.

"Next you must build a small fire outdoors," said Niniu. "When it has burned down to ashes, throw water on it. Scoop up the muddy ashes and soak your kukui in them for two days."

"Two days!" Palani objected. "I won't have any time to learn the trick after I get my top finished!"

"We shall practice with my top while yours is soaking," said Niniu. "If you make your fire tonight and soak your kukui until Wednesday morning, it should have a fine color. That afternoon we can give it a final polishing. Be sure to bring your tooth powder on Wednesday."

"You're joking!" Palani replied. "Why must I brush my teeth before I polish my kukui?"

"We do not brush your teeth, we brush the kukui's teeth!" said Niniu, chuckling. "We need a very fine powder that will not scratch."

The week hurried by. Monday and Tuesday, Palani worked with Niniu's top, learning the Hele Mai trick. On Wednesday afternoon he finished his own top. Thursday and Friday afternoons he worked again at the trick.

"Tomorrow at nine, the contest begins!" said Palani as he was leaving Friday. "I shall come up early for one last practice with you, Niniu. I want to be sure I have that trick just right!"

The sun was barely up when Palani climbed the mountain trail Saturday morning. For a long time he practiced until he could do the Hele Mai without a mistake.
"I am very grateful to you, Niniu!" said Palani. "Whether I win or not, I'll have fun with my kukui top. Mahalo a nui loa!"
"You are welcome," said Niniu. "I learned as much about Yo Yos as you learned about tops. Now I can do the Breakaway, Around the Corner and Over the Falls! Aloha and good luck!"
Palani hurried down the mountain trail with his shining top snug in his pocket. In the valley below he heard the clock on the big Hawaiian church strike nine. The contest was starting! He'd have to hurry or he'd miss it! He began running pell-mell. His foot slipped on a small stone and he went sprawling. He got to his feet, shaken but unhurt. He started running again, but this time he watched the trail.

The playground was crowded when he arrived. Palani hurried over to the judge's stand to have his name checked. He reached into his pocket for his top. A strange look came over his face. There was nothing in his pocket! His kukui nut top was gone! Then he remembered his fall on the trail. The top must have dropped out then and rolled into the bushes! There wasn't time to go back and hunt for it and still get back in time for the contest! He had no other top! He'd just have to withdraw his name!

Slowly, Palani walked over to the judge and explained why he must take his name off the list. Then, discouraged, he wandered over to a big tree near the edge of the playground and sat down. A whole week's work wasted!

In the distance he heard someone call his name. He glanced up. Along the edge of the playground he thought he saw something green moving, then stopping, then moving again. "Just my imagination!" he said.

He covered his eyes with his hands. Across the playground he heard a shout go up for the winner of the first contest. Then he heard his name again. . . .

"Alo—ha, Pala—ni!" That was strange. None of the boys called him that way. Niniu was the only one that used that call. Niniu! Down here? He looked up, startled as he heard a rustling in the grass. There stood Niniu!

"Niniu! What are you doing here?" Palani gasped. "I thought you never came this close to people, especially in the daylight!"

"I don't . . . unless it's something very important," said Niniu, "and this is. How do you expect to win a top contest without a top?" He held out his hand. In the palm lay Palani's kukui top.

"You found it!" cried Palani. "Where was it?"

"Right beside the trail, where you dropped it," said Niniu. "Now hurry! Get back in the contest, wikiwiki!"

"Mahalo again, Niniu!" said Palani, hurrying to the judge's stand. "Will you enter my name again, Judge?" he asked. "I've got my top back."

"I'll be glad to," said the judge. "Where did you find your top?"

"I didn't find it," said Palani honestly. "A menehune brought it back to me."

"So a menehune brought it back to you, eh?" said the judge. "That's a good joke!"

A laugh rippled over the crowd.

Palani laughed too, but he was laughing for a different reason. He was laughing because in all that crowd, he was the only one who knew that a menehune had *really* brought back his kukui nut top.

Menehune Miko

Miko walked slowly toward the entrance of his new school. This was going to be a bad day. He knew just how it would turn out. He'd be the smallest one in second grade. The girls would laugh and the boys would chase him. Just like the first day at his other school, only worse. His new classmates had been together since September and now it was April. A fine time to be changing schools!

The bell hadn't rung yet. Boys and girls were still playing in the school yard. Miko took a deep breath and began whistling as he started up the front walk.

Three boys stopped playing tag to stare.

"You a new kid?" the black-haired one asked.

Miko nodded.

"How come you're so small?" asked the one wearing a cowboy shirt.

Miko grinned. "My grandfather is a menehune."

"Ho ho!" the freckled one jeered. "Let's see if he taught you how to run."

Miko darted off. The three boys were right behind him. Around the building he went and across the playground. At the far end he saw a strip of woods. He headed for that and dashed in among the trees. The three dashed after him.

Branches pulled at him. Roots tripped him. Thorns scratched him. The playground was safer than this, Miko thought. He circled around, found a way out, and hid behind a bush.

From the woods came a sudden yell. The three boys came racing out. They seemed to have forgotten all about Miko. They were running away from something in the woods, and they looked scared!

Miko looked back. At the edge of the woods a little shaggy-haired man in a green malo stood holding his sides and laughing. He was smaller than Miko, with powerful muscles bulging in his arms and legs. He winked, gave a friendly flip of his hand, and disappeared.

The morning went just as Miko had expected. Recess time came. Get ready for more running, Miko thought. Kenji, Lui, and Roy, the three boys who had chased him, circled around him chanting, "Menehune

Miko! Come play hide-and-seek-o!" But they didn't chase him again and they didn't go near the woods.

Two boys were choosing sides for a tug-of-war. One named Emi smiled. "You want to be on our team, Miko?"

Before Miko could answer, another boy yelled, "Hey, Emi! We don't want a little guy like Menehune Miko! Choose somebody strong!"

Miko walked away. But soon he heard Emi calling him. All the ther boys had been chosen and Emi needed one more to even up his team. Miko got on the end of the line.

A teacher asked them to move to the far end of the playground where it was less crowded. The two teams moved. When they lined up again, Miko saw they were close to the woods but there was no sign of the little man in green. No sign of Kenji, Lui, and Roy either, he noticed with a grin.

Emi drew a line on the ground. Everyone grabbed the one ahead of him.

"Ready?" Emi called.

"Ready," the other captain answered.

Everyone pulled. Back and forth the teams see-sawed. Miko felt his feet slipping. Branches rustled behind him and strong arms grabbed him around the waist.

"Hold on!" said the little man. He gave a tremendous tug. Back came the line, so fast that both teams landed in a heap. When Miko got to his feet, the little man had disappeared and Emi was saying, "We won! Now aren't you glad I chose Miko?"

It was the day before May Day. For weeks, classes had been getting ready for a special outdoor program. The girls in Miko's class were doing a hula. Some of the boys were playing for them on split bamboo sticks and gourd rattles. The rest of the boys were doing a tumbling act. They were listed on the program as The Merry Menehunes, and Miko, of course, was one of them.

May Day morning, the second grade boys wore their best slacks, their brightest aloha shirts, and fresh flower leis. So did Miko. The tumblers carried the green malos they would wear later.

When Miko reached his classroom door, the three boys were waiting for him.

"Hey, Menehune Miko! You see that? That's your fault!" Kenji pointed to the heavy fog moving down across the school grounds from Mauna Kea.

"He's right!" said Lui. "We always had a sunny May Day until you came!"

Roy shook his fist. "You better talk to that menehune grandfather of yours and tell him to give us good weather. If our program's spoiled, you'll be sorry!"

Kenji, Lui, and Roy went into the classroom and slammed the door.

The school clock showed five minutes before the first bell. Miko crossed the lawn to see the thrones trimmed with flowers for the May King and Queen. They were set in a cluster of tall tree ferns, and peering out between the fern fronds was the menehune.

Miko took off his flower lei, put it around the little man's neck, and whispered something. The menehune nodded. The first bell rang and Miko, smiling, hurried to class.

By nine o'clock the rows of benches outdoors were filled with parents and small brothers and sisters. All wore their most colorful Hawaiian clothes and all watched the sky anxiously.

The King and Queen came into sight, and the fog began to lift. The first graders came twisting and prancing, and the sky showed blue. The second grade dancers took their places, and the sun broke through the clouds. Everyone clapped and smiled. Miko glanced toward the tree ferns and nodded.

The hula ended. It was time for The Merry Menehunes. Wearing their green malos, they came rolling and tumbling over the grass. They did forward rolls. They did back flips. They did hand stands. They built a six-man pyramid.

Then from opposite sides came two small figures turning perfect cartwheels. Back they came, doing leaping somersaults. Then, grasping each other's ankles, they formed a hoop that went rolling over and over and over. One of the figures was Miko. It was hard to tell who the other was.

The hoop rolled to a stop. As Miko got to his feet, the other tumbler stooped, lifted him by the ankles straight up into the air, and balanced him there. Miko's classmates cheered. He jumped lightly down. Then he and his partner joined the other Merry Menehunes and all went leap-frogging off. A wave of applause swept the audience.

People are still talking about that May Day program and The Merry Menehunes. They are still trying to figure out who Miko's partner could have been.

Miko grins, but doesn't say. He has some good friends at school now. They have found out that he does some things very well and some things not so well—just like everyone else—and size has nothing to do with it.

Nobody calls him Menehune Miko any longer. Most of his classmates have stopped because they no longer think of his being small. Kenji, Lui, and Roy have stopped because they're not taking any chances. They think it might just be true that his grandfather is a menehune!

The Dam That Disappeared

It was the last week of summer camp. The afternoon sun shone down on the Craft Tent, overflowing with boys working hard to finish their model outrigger canoes.

Teo was the youngest camper. Everything seemed strange to him, and a little frightening. His real name was Timoteo, but the boys had started calling him Timid Teo. All but Akoni. Akoni was his good friend, and he was not afraid of anything.

Teo struggled to fasten the outrigger on his canoe. It kept slipping off. "I'll never get this done in time for closing night," he said.

"Sure you will," said Akoni. "Here, I'll help you."

They worked until Big Bill, the camp counselor, announced it was time to clean up and try out the finished canoes.

Akoni grabbed Teo's hand and led the way through the woods and up the rocky path to the top of a small waterfall. Here the stream spread out in a quiet pool at one side of the moving water.

Teo couldn't wait to try out his canoe. He set it in the water and gave it a push. It wobbled, then balanced itself and sailed smoothly across the pool.

"Look! It's floating!" Teo cried.

"Watch out!" Akoni called.

Too late. The canoe had sailed beyond the still water. The swift current was sweeping it toward the waterfall.

Teo cried out, "Catch it, somebody!"

Akoni grabbed a branch and caught the little canoe just before it went over the falls. "We'll have to build a dam before we can sail our canoes here," he said.

"Let's get busy," said Big Bill.

The older boys set to work. Struggling, they pushed heavy stones from the stream bed into a line above the waterfall. Teo stood on the bank watching.

"Teo, find us some small stones to fit in between these," Big Bill called.

Teo hesitated. He moved slowly into the water. It felt cold and scary at first, but soon he was enjoying it. He made two trips, carrying stones to Big Bill. Then he splashed over to where Akoni was working.

"Look what I found, Akoni! A stone with a T on it!" He held out a stone with two white streaks.

"That's T for Teo," said Akoni.

Teo laughed. "Now I'll try to find A for Akoni!" He hunted for a long time. When he came back he said, "I couldn't find one, Akoni, so I marked one for you." He handed him a gray stone with an A scratched on it.

"Thanks," Akoni said. "I'll put these two right here, side by side."

The dam was finished at last. It had been hard work and it had taken every loose stone in sight. Tired and hungry, the boys trooped back to wash up for the evening meal.

Akoni was up early next morning. "Let's go down to the dam before breakfast," he said to Teo. Through the woods and up the rocky path they went. Suddenly they stopped.

The dam was gone! Not a stone remained in place.

Teo started. "What happened? Did the stones wash over the falls?"

"No, they're not down there," said Akoni.

Teo looked frightened. "Maybe menehunes took them away!"

"Menehunes!" Akoni snorted. "More likely it was some of the kids who didn't make canoes. We'll fix it later. Come on, there goes the breakfast bell."

After breakfast, the whole camp turned out to rebuild the dam. But no one could find the stones! Every one of them had disappeared. The boys groaned, thinking of all their hard work wasted. Big Bill, to cheer them up, suggested a hike.

Soon the boys were swinging along the trail, singing a hiking song. After a mile they stopped to rest near a shady hillside.

"Come on, Teo. Let's explore," said Akoni. "There's a cave over there. I want to see what's inside."

"You go in. I'll wait outside for you," Teo said in a small voice.

Akoni crawled through the low entrance. When he came out he looked puzzled. He was holding two stones — one marked T and the other, A.

"Our special stones!" Teo said in a whisper. "How did they get in there?"

Akoni shook his head. "I don't know. The other stones from the dam are in there too. Who could have carried them this far?"

"Menehunes!" Teo squealed.

"No, not menehunes!" said Akoni. "But whoever did move them must have done it after dark. I'll put these back in the cave. Tonight, when everyone's asleep, we'll go down to the stream and watch."

Teo felt scared, but he nodded.

Camp seemed spooky with everything so dark and still.

"Have you got the blanket?" Akoni asked in a whisper.

"Y-y-yes, I've got it," Teo answered.

A single light burned in the counselor's tent as they crept quietly into the woods. In the beam of Akoni's flashlight, the trees had strange faces and long twisty arms.

Teo shivered. "Let's go back, Akoni."

Akoni didn't answer. He just kept on going until they reached the stream. They could hear the water rushing over the falls. The moon came out from behind a cloud. There was no one in sight. The boys huddled in their blanket, peering through the moonlight and listening. The water played a drowsy tune. Soon they dozed, then woke with a start.

A crowd of little men was pouring out of the woods on the far side of the stream. Laughing and calling to each other they plunged into the water. Some swam. Some tossed pebbles and dived after them. Some slid down the waterfall.

Akoni leaned forward to see better. His flashlight rolled down the bank and hit the water with a splash.

In a twinkling, the little men were gone. All but one, who seemed to be the chief. He climbed out of the water and glared at the boys.

"So you're the ones who spoiled our waterfall!" he said.

Teo's mouth popped open. He forgot to be afraid. "You're the ones who spoiled our dam!" he said. "I worked so hard to finish my canoe and now I can't sail it!"

The small chief looked startled. "We didn't know about that," he said. "But this has been one of our favorite spots for a long time. We can't have a dam here!"

"Not even for one night?" Teo pleaded. "Tomorrow's our last night in camp. We were going to have a special ceremony sailing our canoes here."

The menehune chief hesitated. "Wait here," he said gruffly. He swam back across the stream and gave a low whistle.

The little men came swarming out of the woods again and gathered around him. As he spoke to them, they looked across at Teo and Akoni and scowled.

Teo sighed. "They're not going to help us."

Akoni, who hadn't said a word since the little men appeared, stood staring, still unable to believe his eyes.

Suddenly the menehunes plunged into the water and came swimming across. More came pouring out of the shadows to join them. On the near shore they climbed out and formed a single line that stretched from the waterfall off into the woods.

The chief spoke to Teo. "We will rebuild the dam for your ceremony and take it down after camp closes. Now stay out of our way while we work."

Teo nodded. Back on their blanket, he and Akoni watched the busy little men. Along the line came the stones, passing from hand to hand. Down the line they came, to the workers at the waterfall. As if by magic, the dam took shape again. The last two stones in place were those marked T and A. Teo looked at Akoni and grinned.

It was the last night of camp. As the sky grew dark, a torchlight procession came winding through the woods to the pool. Teo and Akoni, with the other canoe builders, took their places at the water's edge.

Big Bill lifted a shell trumpet and blew a long eerie blast. At the signal, Teo felt the hair prickle at the back of his neck. He struck a match and lighted the candle in his small canoe. Along the bank, each boy did the same.

While the candles flickered, the boys sang their farewell to camp. Slowly the fleet of lighted canoes moved out across the still water, each with a secret cargo.

Teo didn't feel timid now. After all, he was the camper who had talked with a menehune chief. He was the camper who had thought of tucking a small ti leaf packet of silvery fish into each canoe — a gift for the little men of the forest who had rebuilt the dam that disappeared.

Glossary

ae (<u>ah</u>-ay) yes
ahi (<u>ah</u>-hee) fire
aikane (<u>ah</u>-ee-kah-nay) friend
Akoni (Ah-<u>ko</u>-nee) Anthony
aloha (ah-<u>lo</u>-hah) greeting or farewell
auwe (<u>ah</u>-oo-<u>way</u>) alas!
calabash (<u>cal</u>-a-bash) bowl made of gourd or wood
Eka (<u>Ay</u>-kah) Edgar
Ele-ele (<u>ay</u>-lay-<u>ay</u>-lay) black; used here as a name
hele mai (<u>hay</u>-lay-<u>mah</u>-ee) come here!
hoihope (<u>ho</u>-ee-<u>ho</u>-pay) back up! reverse!
huki (<u>hoo</u>-key) pull!
huli (<u>hoo</u>-lee) turn!
Kalepa (Kah-<u>lay</u>-pah) storekeeper; used here as a family name
keiki (<u>kay</u>-key) child
Kele (<u>Kay</u>-lay) Jerry
koa (<u>ko</u>-ah) a fine Hawaiian wood
kokua (ko-<u>koo</u>-ah) help
kukui (koo-<u>koo</u>-ee) candlenut tree; its nuts are often made into jewelry or spinning tops

43

Kulolo (Koo-lo-lo) pudding of coconut and taro

lanai (lah-nah-ee) porch, balcony

lei (lay-ee) a garland or necklace of flowers, leaves, nuts, shells or feathers

Luka (Loo-kah) Luke

mahalo (mah-hah-lo) thank you

mahalo a nui loa (mah-hah-lo a noo-ee lo-ah) thank you very much

maikai (mah-ee-kah-ee) good! fine!

maile (mah-ee-lay) fragrant vine; leis of this are highly prized

malo (mah-lo) loin cloth

Mauna Kea (Mah-oo-nah Kay-ah) White Mountain; dormant volcano on island of Hawaii

Mauna Loa (Mah-oo-nah Lo-ah) Long Mountain; active volcano on island of Hawaii

Mele-mele (may-lay-may-lay) yellow; used here as a name

menehune (may-nay-hoo-nay) one of the legendary little people of Hawaii

Moke (Mo-kay) Moses

Niniu (nee-nee-oo) whirl, spin; used here as a name

niu (nee-oo) coconut

nui (noo-ee) big, great

Oka (Oh-kah) Oscar

Palani (Pah-lah-nee) Frank

Peka (Pay-kah) Bert

Pilipo (Pee-lee-po) Philip

plumeria (plu-may-ree-ah) fragrant blossoms used in making leis

Poepoe (Po-ay-po-ay) round; used here as a family name

poi (po-ee) food made from taro root cooked and pounded with water

taro (tah-ro) important vegetable food in Hawaii

ti (tee) plant whose wide, smooth leaves are often used for wrapping food

Timoteo (Tee-mo-tay-o) Timothy

Tutuma (Too-too-mah) Grandmother

Tutupa (Too-too-pah) Grandfather

ulu (oo-loo) breadfruit

waiu (wah-ee-oo) milk

Wene (Way-nay) Wayne

wikiwiki (wee-kee-wee-kee) hurry